LAWS TO LIVE BY
STEPS TO A BETTER LIFE

LEADER'S GUIDE

DR. STEVEN A. JIRGAL

Published by The Core Media Group, Inc., P.O. Box 2037, Indian Trail, NC 28079.

Printed in the United States of America.

Table of Contents

❦

Purpose

❧

This Leader's Guide is meant to be an aid through life. It is in no way meant to replace the Ten Commandments given by Almighty God. The Ten Commandments have been given to us to help us establish social and religious order both as individuals and as a people called by God. *Laws to Live By* is simply a set of ten laws that can guide a person in the direction of better decision-making and thereby give him a better living situation. All biblical references are taken from the New American Standard Bible.

A Word About Teaching

Good Bible Teachers...

A.) Teach by the Spirit of God and let the Spirit of God work through them. God will do this in various ways: Through His Word, circumstances and situations, past experiences, and His Spirit prompting you. With this in mind, it is imperative that you PRAY, PRAY, PRAY.

B.) Take complex concepts and make them simple and understandable, not the other way around. People will come and listen to you teach when you take the information you are trying to convey and put it in a text they can understand. Jesus did this. He took a concept He was trying to give them and connected it through the use of storytelling in a context they could easily grasp. The women around Him understood the value of dowry coins. Men under His teaching knew about sheep. Parents were keyed into raising their children. So, He told them how much value the Heavenly Father placed on them. The parables of the lost coin, lost sheep, and wayward son resonated with them and they could understand the Father's desire to be with them.

A Negative Example
David Evans postulates the military would take the following statement and revise it out of existence:

1st Draft: A word to the wise is sufficient.
2nd Draft: A word to the wise may be sufficient.
3rd Draft: It is believed that a word to the wise may be sufficient.
4th Draft: It is believed by some that a word to the wise may be sufficient under some conditions.
5th Draft: Indications are that it is believed by some that a word to the wise may be sufficient under some conditions, although this may possibly vary under differing circumstances. This conclusion may not be supportable under detailed analysis and should be used only in a general sense with a full realization of the underlying assumptions.

A Positive Example
How does an internal combustion engine work?
Combustion, also known as burning, is the basic chemical process of releasing energy from a fuel and air mixture. In an internal combustion engine (ICE), the ignition and combustion of the fuel occurs within the engine itself. The engine then partially converts the energy from the combustion to work. The engine consists of a fixed cylinder and a moving piston. The expanding combustion gases push the piston, which

in turn rotates the crankshaft. Ultimately, through a system of gears in the powertrain, this motion drives the vehicle's wheels.

Simplified

When you press down on your gas pedal, more gasoline is released into the engine and your car accelerates.

C.) Ask conversational questions that required more than "Yes" and "No" answers. If it's a "Yes" or "No" question it should be followed by the question, "Why do you feel that way?" You must find a way to draw those whom you lead into conversation. Your teaching must be more than a lecture. When people are engaged in conversation over a particular subject, it penetrates their hearts and minds, and it has the best chance of being a life-changing encounter.

D.) Keep current. Be aware of what's happening in others' lives, our society, and the world. File these issues away and draw upon them when applicable.

E.) Prepare early. You teach out of your abundance. The earlier you prepare your lesson, the better you will learn it and the more time you will give the Lord to direct you.

F.) Use illustrations. That's what Jesus did. Matt. 13:34, "All these things Jesus spoke to the crowds in parables, and He did not speak to them without a parable." Keep in mind: "We learn by hearing (exposure). But we remember by illustration." -Dr. Steve Jirgal

G.) Always provide application. "Impression without expression can lead to stagnation." Show those in your charge the "What" followed by the "So what" part of the lesson. It is not enough simply to explain the meaning of a lesson or portion of Scripture. You must always find a way to show your group how the truth you are sharing fits into their lives.

Introduction

No matter where we are in our Christian walk, the goal of our lives should be to move to *the next level*. This is called sanctification or maturation. Next-level living starts by realizing (and accepting) that in each of our lives there is room for improvement.

All of us can relate to the premise: "I can be better at..."Financial management, Friendship, My Walk of Faith, Parenting, Grandparenting, Marriage, Employment Situations, Health Issues, etc.

Rules are important in our lives. They give us Safety/Order/Sane Living.

There are certain universal laws that apply to any age, any stage, and any location. These laws cannot be broken. We only break ourselves against these laws. A few of these laws include gravity, inertia, and the rate of acceleration.

We see these laws exemplified in this way: No two objects can occupy the same space at the same time with one or both being compromised. If you've ever been in a car accident you've experienced this law first-hand.

Follow these universal laws and life will be better.

Disregard these laws and life can become difficult both for you and those around you.

Just as there are universal laws that govern our physical lives, there are other laws that govern our personal lives. Following are ten laws that affect us and those around us in many ways. Understanding and obeying these laws will go a long way toward making our lives better socially, spiritually, and physically.

1

You Become What You Are Surrounded By

Chameleons….. What is most notable about chameleons? They change color to meet their surroundings. This is for their safety and protection, and it is an involuntary reaction. They don't get to pick their colors. The environment does that for them.

Unlike the chameleon, you can pick your colors, because you can pick your environment. The problem arises however, when pick the wrong environment based on the wrong desire. You and I have an innate desire for acceptance-to fit in-to belong. And the natural tendency is to gravitate toward those who accept you. This makes it ever more important to choose the right people to whom we attach ourselves.

Proverbs 1:10-19 gives a clear illustration of this:

> "My son, if sinners entice you, do not consent. [11] If they say, 'Come with us, Let us lie in wait for blood, Let us ambush the innocent without cause; [12] Let us swallow them alive like Sheol, even whole, as those who go down to the pit; [13] We will find all kinds

*of precious wealth, we will fill our houses with spoil; **14 Throw in your lot with us, we shall all have one purse,' 15 my son, do not walk in the way with them. Keep your feet from their path, 16 for their feet run to evil and they hasten to shed blood. 17 Indeed, it is useless to spread the* baited *net in the sight of any bird; 18 But they lie in wait for their own blood; They ambush their own lives. 19So are the ways of everyone who gains by violence; It takes away the life of its possessors."*

Look at and underline the phrases of attraction:

- V.10: "entice-means to lure, like a fish is lured to bait.
- V.11: "Come with us..."
- V.11: "Let us..."
- V.11: "Let us..."
- V.12: "Let us..."
- V.13: "We will..."
- V.13: "We will..."
- V.14: "With us..."
- V.14: "We shall..."

These are all phrases of acceptance and inclusion and carry with them great attraction. However, the road these *friends* are traveling will lead them to a very undesirable destination.

The writer gives a clear directive in verse 15: "my

son, do not walk in the way with them. Keep your feet from their path…"

The advice is clear: *Don't walk with them*. Today's directive would be: *Don't hang out with them*. In fact, it goes further than that: "Keep your feet from their path." Today we would say, *"Don't even go to the places where you know they hang out!"*

Verse 16 tells us, these kinds of people, not only *look* for evil and violence, they *run* to it! Verse 17 tells us they are not even wise enough to see the trouble coming their way. Even a bird avoids a trap when he sees it. Hence the insult "bird brains."

Verse 19 tells us the conclusion of the matter. The activities they are involved with, will in the end, take their life. And, if you are found in their company, it will take your life as well!

We are instructed in Psalm 13:20, "He who walks with wise men will be wise, but the companion of fools will suffer harm."

In 1 Corinthians 15:33 we are told, "Do not be deceived: "Bad company corrupts good morals."

These two verses seem to be the conclusion of Proverbs 1:19.

Notable Quotable: "The things you let into your life determine the way you go out in life."
-Dr. Steve Jirgal

Key Truth: You are the average of your five closest friends.

Ask: Who are your five closest friends? There are very few neutral relationships. Your friends are either lifting you up, or they are bringing you down.

Ask: How many friends of yours would you label, "Sinkers?"

King Solomon gives us a clear example of what can happen when you surround yourself with those who will drag you down. In 1 Kings 11:4-5, we read, "He had seven hundred wives, princesses, and three hundred concubines, and his wives turned his heart away. For when Solomon was old, his wives turned his heart away after other gods; and his heart was not wholly devoted to the Lord his God, as the heart of David his father had been."

Ask: Have you seen examples of people who have had problems because of those they decided to be connected to? Share an example of someone whose connections have lifted them up to a better situation.

Key Truth: As followers of the Lord, we are to have

an impact on our society. Yet the Bible instructs us to closely guard our associations.

---

1 Corinthians 5:9-10 tells us, "I wrote you in my letter not to associate with immoral people; I did not at all mean with the immoral people of this world, or with the covetous and swindlers, or with idolaters, for then you would have to go out of the world."

The people Paul is talking about are those who name the name of Christ. They are the ones who claim to follow the Lord but are living immoral lives.

Also, Romans 12:2, gives us clear direction, "And do not be conformed to this world, but be transformed by the renewing of your mind, so that you may prove what the will of God is, that which is good and acceptable and perfect."

This calls us to **Insulate not Isolate**. We can't avoid contact with those who do not follow the faith and we shouldn't go out of our way to do so. But just like a good doctor does, we must get close enough to treat the *patient*, but not so close that we catch the disease.

Ask: How do you see that phrase lived out in your life?

2

The Choices You Make Today May Determine the Opportunities You Have Tomorrow

---

Key Truth: Choices bring consequences.

Illustration 1

Kenny was an employee of a large security firm in New York City. On a particular day he had several appointments throughout Manhattan. He was usually very prompt and committed to make his appointments on time. On this day, for some reason, he let an appointment slide. He called ahead and cancelled his appointment down in the business district of lower Manhattan. Within two hours the twin towers, where his appointment was located, were destroyed. If Kenny had adhered to his plans, he would have found himself on the second floor when the planes destroyed the buildings. His choice saved his life and allowed him to live another day.

Illustration 2

In 2018, at Moulton Falls Regional Park in the state

of Washington, eighteen year old Taylor Smith made the decision to push her sixteen year old friend off the bridge she was standing on. Jordan Holgerson suffered serious injuries among which were several broken ribs, a bruised esophagus, an injured trachea, and a punctured lung.

Smith's comment was "...I didn't think about the consequences."

She was charged with reckless endangerment and was required to serve time in jail, serve on a work crew, pay a fine, and be restrained from seeing Holgerson for two years.

Ask: What are some obvious things that her choice cost her?

Answer: The loss of a friend...damage to her reputation...financial loss to her family...nationwide criticism...jail time, and a police record from which she will undoubtedly never fully recover.

***Notable Quotable**: "The moment is over in a moment, but what you choose in that moment creates your future." -Katherine Lee*

Illustration 3

John was a freshman in college. One night, when his mother was away for the weekend, he made three inter-connected poor decisions. He decided to have a party, although underage, he chose to bring in alcohol, and he chose to go public with those he invited.

In a very short time, his home was filled with partyers many of whom he had never met. Things quickly got out of hand and a fight broke out. John wound up beating another young man so severely that he had to be hospitalized. John was arrested and charged with multiple violations including und-eraged drinking, supplying alcohol to minors, and assault. He was a clear demonstration that the choices you make today determine the opportunities you have tomorrow. This was revealed to him clearly in his dismissal from school where he was majoring in criminal justice with the goal of working for the FBI.

If sin were not enjoyable, it wouldn't be so hard to resist. Hebrews 11:25 tells us that sin does bring plea-sure, but it is passing enjoyment. In Numbers 32:23 we find the children of Israel preparing to cross the Jordan River and enter the promised land. The tribes Reuben and Gad desired to settle in the land on the near side of the Jordan. They requested from Mo-ses permission to do so. Moses' concern was that the two tribes would not join the other tribes when trouble arose while they took the land. He issues a warning to them we would do well to heed, "But if you will not do so, behold, you have sinned against the Lord, and be sure your sin will find you out."

Key Truth: No one gets away with sin. It may

appear that they do, but the eyes of God see all. And eventually poor decisions fall under the judgment of God.

Regarding decisions that we must make, what you find that will generally happen is good choices bring negative short-term results/reactions, but positive long-term results/reactions. An example of this is when a student stays behind to study instead of going to a party with their friends! At first, he will experience the ridicule of his buddies. But later, when the test grades come back, he very well can experience the satisfaction that comes from making the right choices.

<u>Ask</u>: Have you ever experienced this? Feel free to share.

Bad choices bring positive short-term results/reactions, but negative long-term results/reactions. This is evidenced by those who choose to smoke. At front end, the experience of smoking may bring positive results. They enjoy the taste. It makes them feel grown-up. They find acceptance from other smokers. But when lung disease, heart issues, or cancer shows up in their lives, the benefits fall through the basement.

Ask: How have you seen this displayed in people's lives?

What biblical examples of negative choices can you think of and what were the results? (Adam & Eve, Judas, Lot, the Prodigal Son, Rich man w/ Jesus.)

What positive biblical examples can you think of and what were the results? (Ruth, Esther, Moses, Joseph, Thomas, Noah, Stephen.)

Notable Quotable: "Up to a point a man's life is shaped by environment, heredity, and movements and changes in the world about him. Then there comes a time when it lies within his grasp to shape the clay of his life into the sort of thing he wishes to be. Only the weak blame parents, their race, their times, lack of good fortune, or the quirks of fate. Everyone has it within his power to say, This I am today; that I will be tomorrow." -Louis L'Amour, The Walking Dream._

Key Truth: You can't always choose what happens To You, but you can always choose what happens In You.

It is very important that you recognize when choices are before you. A voice should go off in your head and call out: "Choices...Choices...Choices"

Galatians 5:22-23 (The Fruit of the Spirit): Love, Joy, Peace, Patience, Kindness, Goodness, Faithfulness, Gentleness, Self-Control.

These are character traits that develop in your life as you walk closely with the Spirit of God. You CAN choose to exhibit the fruit of the Spirit!

<u>Ask</u>: Which one of the character traits mentioned in Galatians 5:22-23 do you struggle with exhibiting the most? Why do you think this is?

One for the Fridge
The Road Not Taken

Two roads diverged in a yellow wood,
And sorry I could not travel both
And be one traveler; long I stood
And looked down one as far as I could go
To where it bent in the undergrowth;

Then took the other, as just as fair
And having perhaps the better claim,
Because it was grassy and wanted wear
Though as for that, the passing there
Had worn them really about the same.

And both that morning equally lay,
In leaves no step had trodden black.
Oh, I kept the first for another day!

Yet knowing how way leads on way,
I doubted if I should ever come back.

I shall be telling this with a sigh
Somewhere ages and ages hence;
Two roads diverged in a wood, and I-
I took the one less traveled by,
And that has made all the difference.

-Robert Frost

-3-

People Will Forget What You Say and People Will Forget What You Do, but They Will Never Forget the Way You Made Them Feel
-Maya Angelou

❧

This law can reveal itself in both positive and negative ways. It is possible to treat someone in such a way that you leave an indelible mark on their heart.

It is very likely that the person who coined the adage, *sticks and stones may break my bones, but names will never hurt me* was not on the losing side of that phrase. The fact is, our words have the power to hurt or to heal. This is why teachers are taught to avoid correcting a student in front of his peers! The pain of public embarrassment can last a lifetime.

Illustration 1

Hank is over fifty years old, yet he still remembers the day he got caught passing a note to a friend in class. He was a fairly shy 3rd grader. When Mrs. Rollins (he still remembers her name) intercepted it, she decided to make an example out of him. She drew a small dot on the board and instructed him to stand with his nose on the dot. He stood there for five minutes (it seemed like five hours to him) while his classmates laughed at him. Negative encounters can last a lifetime.

Conversely, positive experiences with others can last just as long.

Illustration 2

A well-known actor was filming a movie in Central Park. There was a point in the filming where a young boy was supposed to approach him and recite a few lines. When the time came, the boy froze. They tried a couple of times, but the young man could not bring himself to face the actor and perform. It ended with the boy in tears. The director wanted to replace the boy, but the actor had other ideas. He told everyone to rehearse around that scene and took the boy aside. They sat at a picnic table and the actor spent some time sharing with the youngster and encouraging him. A short time later, the scene was resumed, and the boy spoke his lines flawlessly. But more than that, I'm certain he came away with great respect and admiration for the actor because he showed that he cared.

<u>Ask</u>: Growing up, who has made you feel good? Who spoke life-giving words into your life? How did they do it?

Too often we forget the Bible's admonitions, "Love

one another." (John 15:12) What a different world we would have if we put into practice the Lord's directive to "Treat others the same way you want them to treat you." (Luke 6:31).

Ask: What Biblical Examples of this law come to mind?

- **Woman to be stoned to death.**
- **Peter, a Tax Collector invited by Jesus to join Him.**
- **Jesus told the little children to come to him.**
- **Samaritans were outcasts and detested by the Jews. Jesus makes a Samaritan the hero of the parable of the "The Good Samaritan."**
- **Onesiphorus-His name means "Profit Bearer"**
- **God's Messenger Angel-He speaks to the women at the empty tomb and instructs them to tell the disciple *and Peter* that they would see Jesus in Galilee. (Peter must have marveled that the angel specifically mentioned his name.)**

Women held a very low status position in New Testament times. In fact, women were in some ways considered property. It was said that a woman was incapable of telling the truth; therefore, women were not allowed to testify in court. Yet, the very first missionaries were women returning from the empty tomb. What a shift in the cultural norm.

Lepers were the *Untouchables* of their society. To be judged a leper meant immediate banishment from public contact. Lepers were instructed to stay fifty feet away from those not infected. If a crowd approached, they were to call out, "Unclean! Unclean!" It protected others from contact, but I'm sure it also reminded every leper of his plight. But in Matt. 8:3, we learn that Jesus *TOUCHED* a leper and healed him. Perhaps this particular leper had not been touched by anyone in a very long time. Jesus touched him! Jesus healed him! Jesus forever changed his life! And I'm certain the leper never forgot the touch of the master's hand.

Encouragement is said to be *Medicine for the Soul*. So many of us can relate to that statement, and we might know someone that could use a good dose of encouragement. The right word, at the right time, just might change someone's entire life! Without question, a person like Teddy Stallard can. In Elizabeth Silance Ballard's fictional story of Teddy Stallard, she writes:

> *Teddy Stallard certainly qualified as "one of the least." Disinterested in school with musty, wrinkled clothes; hair never combed. One of those kids in school with a deadpan face, expressionless-sort of a glassy, unfocused stare. When Miss Thompson spoke to Teddy, he always answered in monosyllables. Unattractive, unmotivated, and distant, he was just plain hard to like. Even*

though his teacher said she loved all in her class the same, down inside she wasn't being completely truthful.

Whenever she marked Teddy's papers, she got a certain perverse pleasure out of putting X's next to the wrong answers, and when she put F's at the top of the papers, she always did it with a flair. She should have known better; she had Teddy's records and she knew more about him than she wanted to admit. The records read:

1st Grade: Teddy shows promise with his work and attitude, but poor home situation.

2nd Grade: Teddy could do better. Mother is seriously ill. He receives little help at home.

3rd Grade: Teddy is a good boy but too serious. He is a slow learner. His mother died last year.

4th Grade: Teddy is very slow, but well-behaved. His father shows no interest.

Christmas came, and the boys and girls in Miss Thompson's class brought her Christmas presents. They piled their presents on her desk and crowded around to watch her open them. Among the presents there was one from Teddy Stallard. She was surprised that he had brought her a gift, but he had. Teddy's gift was wrapped in brown paper and was held together with Scotch tape. On the paper were written the simple words, "For Miss Thompson from Teddy." When she opened Teddy's present, out fell a gaudy rhinestone bracelet, with half the stones missing, and a bottle of cheap perfume.

The other boys and girls began to giggle and smirk over Teddy's gifts, but Miss Thompson at least had enough sense to silence them by immediately putting on the bracelet and putting some of the perfume on her wrist. Holding her wrist up for the other children to smell, she said, "Doesn't it smell lovely?" And the children, taking their cue from the teacher, readily agreed with "oohs" and "ahhs."

At the end of the day, when school was over and the other children had left, Teddy lingered behind. He slowly came over to her desk and said softly, "Miss Thompson... Miss Thompson, you smell just like my mother... and her bracelet looks real pretty on you, too. I'm glad you liked my presents." When Teddy left, Miss Thompson got down on her knees and asked God to forgive her.

The next day when the children came to school, they were welcomed by a new teacher. Miss Thompson had become a different person. She was no longer just a teacher; she had become an agent of God. She was now a person committed to loving her children and doing things for them that would live on after her. She helped all the children, but especially the slow ones, and especially Teddy Stallard. By the end of that school year Teddy showed dramatic improvement. He had caught up with most of the students and was even ahead of some.

She didn't hear from Teddy for a long time. Then one day, she received a note that read:

Dear Miss Thompson:

I wanted you to be the first to know.
I will be graduating second in my class.

Love,
Teddy Stallard

Four years later, another note came:

Dear Miss Thompson:

They just told me I will be graduating first in my class. I wanted you to be the first to know. The university has not been easy, but I liked it.

Love,
Teddy Stallard

And four years later:

Dear Miss Thompson:

As of today, I am Theodore Stallard, M.D. How about that? I wanted you to be the first to know. I am getting married next month, the 27th to be exact. I want you to come and sit where my mother would sit if she were alive. You are the only family I have now; Dad died last year.

Love,
Teddy Stallard

Miss Thompson went to that wedding and sat where Teddy's mother would have sat. She deserved to sit there; she had done something for Teddy that he could never forget.

What can you give as a gift? Instead of shopping and buying something for someone in need, go deeper and farther. Give something that will live on after you and change a life. Give yourself to a real

Teddy Stallard. You can bring them from the bottom and raise them to the top.

Ask: What are some simple ways you can make a difference in someone's life as you go about your everyday tasks?

- **Holding a door.**
- **Remembering a name.**
- **Shaking a hand.**
- **Writing a note.**
- **Giving a smile or hug.**
- **Sharing a simple compliment.**
- **Making a short phone call.**

Key Truth: It takes very little time and effort to make a profound difference in someone's life.

Notable Quotable: "Flatter me and I may not believe you. Criticize me and I may not like you. Ignore me and I may not forgive you. Encourage me and I will not forget you." -William Arthur Ward

---

-4-

Time Is Limited

❦

Ask: Who is the oldest here? Who has the oldest living relative? How old?

It is very possible that most of our lives are behind us!

The question is, what will you do with the rest of it?

Illustration 1

Alfred Nobel and his brother invented dynamite and other weapons of destruction. After his brother Ludvig died, he was shocked upon reading his brother's obituary. The newspaper had inadvertently mixed his brother's obituary with Alfred's. Alfred was in fact, reading his own obituary. This shook him to the core. He did not want his legacy to be filled with destruction and violence, and he decided to do something about it. He invested his money in those who would bring about peace and goodwill to others. This developed into *The Nobel Peace Prize.*

We are all different in so many ways, yet we all have only 24 hours in a day, 1,440 seconds/day, & 525,600 seconds/year.

Someone has said, "We all leave our marks in the sands of time, some leave the mark of a soul, while others leave the mark of a heel."

In John 9:4 we read, "We must work the works of Him who sent Me as long as it is day; night is coming when no one can work."

Illustration 2: A Second Chance

In II Kings 20:1-11, we learn about one of Judah's Kings, Hezekiah. He developed an infection which could not be healed. God sent word through Isaiah that he should get his affairs in order for he would not recover. Hezekiah cried out to the Lord and the Lord granted his desire and extended his life another fifteen years. He got a new lease on life and for the most part used them in honoring God.

Ask: What do you know about the biblical character Caleb?

Another great example of one determined to make a difference by being proactive with his life is seen in the story of Caleb. Caleb was one of the twelve spies sent by Moses to survey the land the Lord would be giving to His people. He and Joshua had confidence that the Lord would certainly deliver the land into the hands of God's people. But they were overruled by the other ten and the children of Israel were destined to wander from place to place until that generation died out. Years later, after taking the land, Joshua was saddled with the task of dividing the territory among the different tribes. At this point, Caleb is eighty-five years old. He approached Joshua with a very unusual request. Joshua 14:6-12, tells of the encounter:

"Then the sons of Judah drew near to Joshua in Gilgal, and Caleb the son of Jephunneh the Kenizzite said to him, 'You know the word which the Lord spoke to Moses the man of God concerning you and me in Kadesh-barnea. ⁷I was forty years old when Moses the servant of the Lord sent me from Kadesh-barnea to spy out the land, and I brought word back to him as it was in my heart. ⁸Nevertheless my brethren who went up with me made the heart of the people melt with fear; but I followed the Lord my God fully. ⁹So Moses swore on that day, saying, 'Surely the land on which your foot has trodden will be an inheritance to you and to your children forever, because you have followed the Lord my God fully.' ¹⁰ Now behold, the Lord has let me live, just as He spoke, these forty-five years, from the time that

the Lord spoke this word to Moses, when Israel walked in the wilderness; and now behold, I am eighty-five years old today. ¹¹ I am still as strong today as I was in the day Moses sent me; as my strength was then, so my strength is now, for war and for going out and coming in. ¹² Now then, give me this hill country about which the Lord spoke on that day, for you heard on that day that Anakim were there, with great fortified cities; perhaps the Lord will be with me, and I will drive them out as the Lord has spoken.'"

<u>Ask</u>: **What jumps out at you from that story?**

<u>Key points:</u>
- **Caleb was eighty-five years old**
- **God promised to give the land to Joshua and Caleb and their descendants.**
- **Caleb still felt strong and vibrant.**
- **The cities he desired were strong and fortified.**
- **The Anakim (giants) occupied these cities.**
- **He was still counting on the Lord to bring the victory.**

<u>Ask</u>: **Everyone preaches their own funeral...What do you want said about you?**

Over time, the character of men and women is revealed. By scanning the Word of God, we see the character of three successive kings unveiled by their choices. Saul showed that he really didn't have a heart for God. David was *sold out* for the Lord and was given the title, *A Man After God's Own Heart* (I Sam. 13:14). Solomon was a man who started well and was full of zeal for God but fell into compromise due to his many relationships with foreign women and the influence of their cultures (I Kings 11:3).

Some key characteristics of those having a positive impact on others include Loving, Peaceful, Faithful, Obedient, Helpful, Wise, Kind, Sacrificial, Hard-Working, Friendly, Generous, Sympathetic, Available, Encouraging.

<u>Ask</u>: If you could pick three qualities you would want to be known by, what would they be?

Psalm. 90:12 tells us, "So teach us to number our days, that we may present to You a heart of wisdom."

In Ecclesiastes. 12:1 we find these words, "Remember also your Creator in the days of your youth, before the evil days come and the years draw near when you will say, 'I have no delight in them.'"

In the movie *Braveheart*, William Wallace is about to lead his Scottish Warriors into battle. He faces them and declares, "Every man dies, not every man lives."

__Notable Quotable__: "Only one life, 'twill soon be past; only what's done for Christ will last."
-C.T. Studd

__Key Truth__: Today is the best day to decide what you will do for the rest of your life. Making a living is vitally important, but making a difference is miles ahead.

The Real Measure of a Person Is Their Character

❧

Our world is filled with examples of false measures of success. Money, possessions, position, connections, experiences, and stature are just some examples of what so many will use to declare a person a success.

Illustration 1

In Charlotte there stands a large and beautiful house. From the outside it oozes *significance*. But that is only a façade. Upon entering the house, you will be surprised to find that the house contains almost no furniture! The couple that lives there can be labeled *house poor*. They have spent all of their money on this expensive home and had little left to fill it with the things they needed to live well inside.

That's the way it is with many people. On the outside, their lives seem to be together, and they seem to be a success. But inside, they are devoid of the things that really make a person a success.

God's standard of success is very different from those in our society. I Samuel 16:7, But the Lord said to Samuel, "Do not look at his appearance or at the height of his stature, because I have rejected him; for God *sees* not as man sees, for man looks at the outward appearance, but the Lord looks at the heart."

Illustration 2

Keeping up with the Jones' used to mean that you compared yourself and the things you had with those who were literally next door. But due to technological advances, the *Jones'* can be found around the globe.

Illustration 3

Better Homes and Gardens is a well-known magazine. Did you ever wonder about the title? Better? Better than what? The answer may be, "Better than yours!"

Some people have character, some people are characters! A person can be a great doctor, but a poor neighbor. Someone can make a lot of money but can't make friends. A man may be able to fix cars but can't fix his family. The great disconnect here is found in one word: Character.

<u>Ask</u>: How would you define character?

When dealing with the topic of character-a humorous side note can be made: One day several angels were looking down from heaven on the people of earth. They looked so discouraged. A lead angel approached them and asked what was troubling them. They explained that they had been surveying the people and noticed that no one was doing what was right. No one was showing any signs of character development. The lead angel said, "I have noticed that as well and have plan for character development among the people. We will find one person who displays positive character traits and reward him with a plaque. The others will see it, be encouraged, and begin to develop their character in positive ways as well." So that's what they did. And do you know what the plaque said? (When no-one answers, say) "I didn't think you'd know, I didn't get one either."

Key Truth: There are moments in our lives when we have to make a choice between going God's way and going our own way. These are the moments when our character is either shaped or revealed.

Ask: Can you share a moment in your life when you were at a juncture and had to make a decision regarding which way you would go?

A person's character is pushed to the surface and revealed in two ways:

A.) When Pressure Comes

A lack of character is easily seen in the life of King Saul. The pressure of a battle with the Philistines added to the pressure of being the first king of Israel. King Saul displayed jealousy, anger and lack of trust (I Sam. 18:6-11):

> "It happened as they were coming, when David returned from killing the Philistine, that the women came out of all the cities of Israel, singing and dancing, to meet King Saul, with tambourines, with joy and with musical instruments. ⁷ The women sang as they played, and said, 'Saul has slain his thousands, And David his ten-thousands.' ⁸ Then Saul became very angry, for this saying displeased him; and he said, 'They have ascribed to David ten-thousands, but to me they have ascribed thousands. Now what more can he have but the kingdom?' ⁹ Saul looked at David with suspicion from that day on. ¹⁰ Now it came about on the next day that an evil spirit from God came mightily upon Saul, and he raved in the midst of the house, while David was playing the harp with his hand, as usual; and a spear was in Saul's hand. ¹¹ Saul hurled the spear for he thought, 'I will pin David to the wall.' But David escaped from his presence twice."

Saul revealed a lack of trust in the Lord (I Sam 13:5-14):

"Now the Philistines assembled to fight with Israel, 30,000 chariots and 6,000 horsemen, and people like the sand which is on the seashore in abundance; and they came up and camped in Michmash, east of Beth-aven. ⁶ When the men of Israel saw that they were in a strait (for the people were hard-pressed), then the people hid themselves in caves, in thickets, in cliffs, in cellars, and in pits. ⁷ Also some of the Hebrews crossed the Jordan into the land of Gad and Gilead. But as for Saul, he was still in Gilgal, and all the people followed him trembling. ⁸ Now he waited seven days, according to the appointed time set by Samuel, but Samuel did not come to Gilgal; and the people were scattering from him. ⁹ So Saul said, 'Bring to me the burnt offering and the peace offerings.' And he offered the burnt offering. ¹⁰ As soon as he finished offering the burnt offering, behold, Samuel came; and Saul went out to meet him and to greet him. ¹¹ But Samuel said, 'What have you done?' And Saul said, 'Because I saw that the people were scattering from me, and that you did not come within the appointed days, and that the Philistines were assembling at Michmash, ¹² therefore I said, 'Now

the Philistines will come down against me at Gilgal, and I have not asked the favor of the Lord.' So I forced myself and offered the burnt offering.' ¹³ Samuel said to Saul, 'You have acted foolishly; you have not kept the commandment of the Lord your God, which He commanded you, for now the Lord would have established your kingdom over Israel forever. ¹⁴ But now your kingdom shall not endure. The Lord has sought out for Himself a man after His own heart, and the Lord has appointed him as ruler over His people, because you have not kept what the Lord commanded you.'"

Ask: **What are the issues in your life you feel pressure over? On a scale of 1-10, how would you rate yourself under these pressures? What are the emotions that most come out of you when the pressure mounts?**

B.) When Opportunity Comes
Two opposing examples:

Ask: **What do you know about the biblical character Gahezi?**

1.) GAHEZI: II-Kings 5:20-25

Background: Elisha is God's prophet. He has a servant named Gehazi.

Naaman is captain of the army of the king of Aram. He is a leper. He comes to Elisha for healing and he is healed. He wants to reward Elisha but the prophet refuses.

But Elisha's servant Gehezi has a plan! He catches up to Naaman.

- He lies to him.
- He lies about Elisha.
- He receives what is not meant for him.
- He returns and lies to Elisha (THE PROPHET).

His character led him down a path resulting in punishment (leprosy) for the rest of his life. (II Kings 5:27)

<u>Ask</u>: Have you ever met someone whose negative character traits caused them great pain? Explain.

2.) JOSEPH: Genesis 37:5-10, 28, 39:4-12

Joseph was given a vision from God that he was to become a great leader. He was to rise above his brothers and even rule over his parents. He was seventeen years old (Genesis. 37:2) when he was taken to Egypt and sold into slavery. While a slave, he rose to prominence in Potiphar's house. He was in charge of all the affairs of the Egyptian leader.

Joseph is a very handsome young man. (Genesis. 39:6). One day, while alone in Potiphar's house, he is approached by Potiphar's wife who wants to have a sexual fling with him.

Ask: What are some of the thoughts that ran through this young man's mind?

- **She wants me!**
- **We are alone. No one will know.**
- **She wants me!!**
- **This is her choice.**
- **Just this once.**
- *Finally!* **I'll get a break and have some pleasure!**
- **If I don't, I'll get in trouble (which is what happened).**
- **She wants me!!!!**

Ask: What was Joseph's response? (Genesis. 39:9-12)

Notable Quotable: *"Fame is a vapor, popularity an accident, and riches take wings. Only one thing endures and that is character."*
-Horace Greeley

With this in mind, we should concentrate on two things:

1.) Change how we view others. Look to their

character rather than their possessions or position.

2.) Concentrate on acquiring desirable character traits. This is a choice!

Key Truth: Each of us is in complete control of the development of our character. As we face decision after decision, we are developing character traits that will shape who we really are.

Notable Quotable: "What you do when you don't have to, will determine what you'll be when you can't help it."

Illustration 4: The Catch of A Lifetime

He was 11 years old and went fishing every chance he got from the dock at his family's cabin on an island in the idle of New Hampshire Lake.

One the day before the bass season opened, he and his father were fishing early in the evening, catching sunfish and perch with worms. Then he tied on a small silver lure and practiced casting. The lure struck the water and cased colored ripples in the sunset, then silver ripples as the moon rose over the lake.

When his pole doubled over, he knew something huge was on the other end. His father watched with admiration as the boy skillfully worked the fish alongside the dock.

Finally, he very gingerly lifted the exhausted fish

from the water. It was the largest one he had ever seen, but it was a bass.

The boy and his father looked at the handsome fish, gills playing back and forth in the moonlight. The father lit a match and looked at his watch. It was 10 P.M.—two hours before the season opened. He looked at the fish, then at the boy.

"You'll have to put it back, Son," he said.

"Dad!" cried the boy.

"There will be other fish," said the father.

"Not as big as this one," cried the boy.

He looked around the lake. No other fishermen or boats were anywhere around in the moonlight. He looked again at his father.

Even though no one had seen them, nor could anyone ever know what time he caught the fish, the boy could tell by the clarity of his father's voice that the decision was not negotiable. He slowly worked the hook out of the lip of the huge bass and lowered it into the black water.

The creature swished its powerful body and disappeared. The boy suspected that he would never again see such a great fish.

That was 34 years ago. Today, the boy is a successful architect in New York City. His father's cabin is still there on the island in the middle of the lake. He takes his own son and daughters fishing from the same dock.

And he was right. He has never again caught such a magnificent fish as the one he landed that night long ago. But he does see the same fish—again and again—every time he comes up against a question of ethics.

For, as his father taught him, ethics are simple matters of right and wrong. It is only the practice of ethics that is difficult. Do we do right when no one is looking? Do we refuse to cut corners to get the design in on time? Or refuse to trade stocks based on information that we know we aren't supposed to have?

We would if we were taught to put the fish back when we were young. For we would have learned the truth.

The decision to do right lives fresh ad fragrant in our memory. It is a story we will proudly tell our friends and grandchildren. Not about how we had a chance to beat the system and took it, but about how we did the right thing and were forever strengthened.

- James P. Lenfestey

-6-

Happiness Is a Choice

Hunger: a biological response.
Pain: a physical condition.
Fever: a protective reaction.
Happiness is an emotion! No one can give it to you!

Notable Quotable: _(Attributed to Abraham Lincoln) "Most folks are usually about as happy as they make up their minds to be."_

It comes down to *PERSPECTIVE*.
In our day, a common statement made by Christians is "God wants me to be happy!"

Ask: What do you think about that philosophy?

It's interesting that the above philosophy only seems to apply to the person who is making the statement. It doesn't apply to the ones they are hurting in the process of their pursuit of happiness.

Key Truth: Happiness and holiness are not the same.

Key Truth: God is more concerned with your holiness than your happiness!

Notable Quotable: "Happiness is the residue of holiness." -Dr. Steve Jirgal

---

Happiness is determined by your perspective regarding your circumstances.

Notable Quotable: "Pain is inevitable, but misery is optional. -Tim Hansel

---

Happiness is a choice based on your viewpoint. It is not an accurate statement to say: "He makes me so mad!" "She makes me smile!" "She makes me so frustrated!" "He makes me feel secure!" No-one can *make* you feel a certain way!

An Elementary school boy in a wheelchair was asked by a visitor, "How are you doing?" His response: "I've got no complaints!"

Key Truth: When trying circumstances come, you can choose to be bitter or choose to get better!

II Cor. 10:5 "We are destroying speculations and every lofty thing raised up against the knowledge of God, and we are taking every thought captive to the obedience of Christ,"

Notable Quotable: "I shall allow no man to belittle my soul by making me hate him." -Booker T. Washington

Suggestions (Not guarantees):

A.) Be thankful for what you have (Not emphasizing what you don't.)
Dr. Seuss (Theodore Seuss Geisel): "Don't be sad because it's over. Be happy because it happened."

Ask: What are the things you have in your life that bring thankfulness to your mind? What do you have that no one can ever take away?

I Tim. 6:6, "But godliness actually is a means of great gain when accompanied by contentment."
Phil. 4:11, Not that I speak from want, for I have

learned to be content in whatever circumstances I am."

B.) Forgive others and embrace forgiveness.

In Genesis. 45:4-8 we find that Joseph had learned to embrace this concept:

> *"Then Joseph said to his brothers, 'Please come closer to me.' And they came closer. And he said, 'I am your brother Joseph, whom you sold into Egypt. ⁵ Now do not be grieved or angry with yourselves, because you sold me here, for God sent me before you to preserve life. ⁶ For the famine has been in the land these two years, and there are still five years in which there will be neither plowing nor harvesting. ⁷ God sent me before you to preserve for you a remnant in the earth, and to keep you alive by a great deliverance. ⁸ Now, therefore, it was not you who sent me here, but God; and He has made me a father to Pharaoh and lord of all his household and ruler over all the land of Egypt.'"*

We also see this in the encounter between Esau and Jacob in Genesis. 27:41, Genesis. 33:4. Jacob had cheated his brother out of both his inheritance and his father's blessing:

> *"So, Esau bore a grudge against Jacob be-*

cause of the blessing with which his father had blessed him; and Esau said to himself, 'The days of mourning for my father are near; then I will kill my brother Jacob.'"

Later in life, the two brothers meet. The reaction Esau had for his brother is surprising:

"Then Esau ran to meet him and embraced him, and fell on his neck and kissed him, and they wept."

We know that God also possesses the ability to forgive. 1 John 1:9, "If we confess our sins, He is faithful and righteous to forgive us our sins and to cleanse us from all unrighteousness."

C.) Invest yourself in helping others

Notable Quotable: "Great men are meteors that consume themselves to light up the earth." -Napoleon

Ask: How did each of the following people serve someone else?

- **AN UNNAMED SLAVE GIRL: helps Naaman be healed of his leprosy - II Kings 5:2-3**
- **ONESIPHORUS: served Paul - II Tim. 1:16**
- **MORDECCI: served Esther - Esther 2:5-7 and**

ESTHER: served God's people - Esther 4:15-16
- **AARON & HURR: served Moses - Exodus 17:12**
- **REBEKAH: served Abraham's servant - Genesis. 24:15-20**

**Notable Quotable**: "Joy is not a feeling; it is a choice. It is not based upon circumstances; it is based upon attitude. It is free, but it is not cheap. It is the by-product of a growing relationship with Jesus Christ. It is a promise, not a deal. It is available to us when we make ourselves available to Him. It is something that we can receive by invitation and by choice. It requires commitment, courage and endurance. And there is no box made by God nor us, but that the top can be blown off and the sides flattened out to make a dance floor on which to celebrate life." -Tim Hansel

<u>Ask</u>: Have your sins been forgiven? Are you saved from the penalty of your sins? Is your place in heaven secured? Has God rescued your soul? Is the Holy Spirit of God dwelling in your heart? Then tell your face and choose to be happy!

-7-

The Scoreboard Is Not the Only Measure of Victory

<u>Ask</u>: How do people in general measure the success of a person? (Possessions, appearance, position, finances)

Those who are deeply involved in athletics know that it is possible to win on the scoreboard but not completely enjoy the victory because of the effort or style of play. Likewise, they have experienced times when the scoreboard displayed a loss, but they *felt* like it was a win because of their effort and the way they played.

This is true in marriage as well. Marital success is **NOT** shown by longevity or the acquiring of things. That can be said to be the world's *scoreboard*. It is possible to have a lot to live on but have little to live for.

Two questions can be used to measure marital success:

1.) Would you marry that person again?

2.) Do you want your children/grandchildren to have the marriage that you have?

Key Truth: Just as marital success cannot be determined by length or possessions, success in life cannot be measured by the standards of the world.

Notable Quotable: (Bumper sticker) "He who dies with the most toys wins."

Additional bumper sticker: "He who dies with the most toys is still dead!"

Key Truth: You can have success in the world's eyes but not in God's eyes.

Example: Exodus 20:7-12:

"'Take the rod; and you and your brother Aaron assemble the congregation and speak to the rock before their eyes, that it may yield its water. You shall thus bring forth water for them out of the rock and let the congregation and their beasts drink.' [9] So Moses took the rod from before the Lord, just as He had commanded him; [10] and Moses and Aaron gathered the assembly before

the rock. And he said to them, 'Listen now, you rebels; shall we bring forth water for you out of this rock?' ¹¹ Then Moses lifted up his hand and struck the rock twice with his rod; and water came forth abundantly, and the congregation and their beasts drank. ¹² But the Lord said to Moses and Aaron, 'Because you have not believed Me, to treat Me as holy in the sight of the sons of Israel, therefore you shall not bring this assembly into the land which I have given them.'"

The children of Israel were wandering in the wilderness. They were suffering from lack of water. Moses and Aaron brought water from the rock. Invariably, the people cheered and indulged in the life-saving maneuver. Moses and Aaron were lifted up in the eyes of the people (the world). BUT, God issued strong condemnation on the pair. The problem was not what they did (the people really did need water). The condemnation came as a result of the way they did it.

- They were told to speak to the rock. They struck the rock (twice).
- They used the phrase, must we bring water from this rock. This placed them at the center of the miracle. In Isaiah 42:8 God states, "I am the Lord, that is my name; I will not give my glory to another, nor my praise to graven images."

<u>Ask</u>: How will you measure your success in life? How do you measure your success or progress as a Christian?

Developing a life philosophy as well as a house are important steps toward ensuring that you are on the winning side of the equation. These philosophies can keep you anchored when life presses in on you and confusion threatens to side-track you.

An example of a Christian life philosophy might include things like:

- Life is not all about me. I belong to God Almighty.
- I am put on this earth to grow in my faith in Jesus Christ so as to live it out in such a way that others will see and want the faith that I have.
- The gifts and talents that I have are to be used to glorify God and to win others to His side.
- I am a child of the King. This means that I should act in a way that honors Him.
- I must commit to treat others the way I want to be treated and to love those who come my way the same way I would have others love me.

An example of a house philosophy might include these things:

- Regarding the authority of your home. (God and God's word)
- Regarding how you treat others. (People matter more than things.)
- Regarding winning:
  1. Doing your best.
  2. Playing by the rules.
  3. Not quitting.
- Regarding worship.

Ask: Are there other areas you can think of to include in a house philosophy?

Notable Quotable: "The price of success is hard work, dedication to the job at hand, and the determination that whether we win or lose, we have applied the best of ourselves to the task at hand." -Vince Lombardi (Coached the Green Bay Packers: 1959-1967. Won the first 2 super bowls and never had a losing season).

Develop a statement regarding what's important in your life with the following suggestions:
- Glorifying God.
- Loving and providing for your family.
- Living out your Christian faith with authenticity.
- Giving.
- Use of talents.

- Dealing honestly with others.
- Displaying love and forgiveness.

Keys to Christian Victory

1.) Obedience: Luke 5:1-5, Although they were seasoned fishermen and had fished all night, (catching nothing), the disciples dropped their net over the side of the boat because Jesus told them to. They simply obeyed.

2.) Faith: II Kings 17:10-16, A famine had hit the land. A woman was down to her last meal. She had a little oil and flour left and was planning on making her and her son a last meal before starvation would overtake them. Then Elijah came along. He too was hungry. He asked the woman to make him a small loaf of bread first

3.) Sacrifice: In Mark 12:41-44, we read of Jesus being with His disciples in the temple. He is drawing their attention to those who are putting their offering into the temple treasury. Some are putting in great amounts of money. Then he points them toward a poor widow who placed two small copper coins (1/64th of a day's wage) in the plate. Jesus commended the woman noting her genuine sacrifice.

Ask: What should our attitude be regarding:
- **Our "Bucket List?"**
- **Life-Long Goals?**

- **Education and career pursuits?**
- **Possessions?**
- **Talents and Abilities?**

For the Fridge

"This is the beginning of a new day. God has given me this day to use as I will. I can waste it or use it for good. What I do today is very important because I am exchanging a day of my life for it. When tomorrow comes, this day will be gone forever, leaving something in its place I have traded for it. I want it to be a gain, not a loss — good not evil. Success, not failure, in order that I shall not regret the price I paid for it."

-Heartsill Wilson

-8-

Wisdom Is a Precious Commodity

A very wise man lived in the hills above a small village. The man was known for his wisdom and was often sought out by those in the village. Knowing this, a young boy and a couple of his friends decided to fool the old man. One of the boys held a small live bird in his hands. His plan was to approach the man and ask if the bird was alive or dead. If the wise man said the bird was alive, he would crush it. If he said it was dead, he would release the bird and prove beyond doubt that the old man was wrong.

When the boy and his friends stood before the sage, they explained that a bird was in the lead boy's hands. They asked him directly, "Is the bird in his hands dead or alive?" The old man sat silently for a moment and then quietly replied, "The answer is in your own hands."

<u>Ask</u>: Do you know anyone who you would consider wise? How have they affected your life?

Is there a difference between being educated

and being wise? If so, what would you say is the difference?

In 1 Kings 3:7-13 Solomon finds himself in the presence of God. The Lord commands him to ask for what he wished from the Almighty. Of all the things Solomon could have asked for, he asked for wisdom:

> *"Now, O Lord my God, You have made Your servant king in place of my father David, yet I am but a little child; I do not know how to go out or come in. ⁸ Your servant is in the midst of Your people which You have chosen, a great people who are too many to be numbered or counted. ⁹ So give Your servant an understanding heart to judge Your people to discern between good and evil. For who is able to judge this great people of Yours?"*

> *¹⁰ It was pleasing in the sight of the Lord that Solomon had asked this thing. ¹¹ God said to him, 'Because you have asked this thing and have not asked for yourself long life, nor have asked riches for yourself, nor have you asked for the life of your enemies, but have asked for yourself discernment to understand justice, ¹² behold, I have done according to your words. Behold, I have*

given you a wise and discerning heart, so that there has been no one like you before you, nor shall one like you arise after you. 13 I have also given you what you have not asked, both riches and honor, so that there will not be any among the kings like you all your days.'"

The following passages of Scripture describe Solomon's wisdom and point out how fully God granted his request:

1 Kings 4:30, "Solomon's wisdom surpassed the wisdom of all the sons of the east and all the wisdom of Egypt."

1 Kings 4:34, "Men came from all peoples to hear the wisdom of Solomon, from all the kings of the earth who had heard of his wisdom."

1 Kings 5:12, "The Lord gave wisdom to Solomon, just as He promised him; and there was peace between Hiram and Solomon, and the two of them made a covenant."

Solomon's wisdom was unparalleled. The fame of his brilliance was so great that a term is used even today of someone whom we would characterize as wise. It's called, "Solomonic wisdom."

1 Kings 3:16-28 demonstrates his wisdom when

two women come to him wanting a ruling regarding a baby.

There is a distinct difference between one who is a fool, one who is smart, and the person who is truly wise: Fools are easy to spot. They are frequently bruised, broke, battling, and blaming all their misfortune on somebody else. Smart people, however, make mistakes but learn from each of their missteps.

But the truly wise observe others and learn from the mistakes they have made.

Share with us a mistake you've made and what lesson(s) you learned from it.

Share something you've learned from observing someone else's mistakes.

Here are some helpful hints for obtaining wisdom:

1.) *Admit that you need it.* Don't be a know-it-all.

2.) *Ask God for it.* James 1:5 tells us, "But if any of you lacks wisdom, let him ask of God, who gives to all generously and without reproach, and it will be given to him."

3.) *Develop an inquisitive mind (Ask Questions).* You will be surprised at the number of people who will gladly share with you their successes and failures.

4.) *Enjoy and generous portion of "PIE."* Expose yourself to people, information, and experiences. (read & listen)

5.) *Work for it.* Unlike Solomon, wisdom most likely, will not just show up on your doorstep. You must go out and get it. Commit yourself to be a life-long learner.

-9-

People Matter More Than Things

The following exercise demonstrates the real importance of things vs. people. It will put things in proper perspective.

Ask your group to:
- Name the winner of 2010 Super Bowl: (Saints Over Colts 31-17)
- Name the #1 movie of the year for 2010: (Argo)
- Name the #1 best-selling car for 2016: (Toyota Camry)

Now:
- Name your Kindergarten teacher.
- Tell your mom or dad's nickname.
- Name your best friend growing up.

In all likelihood, those in your circle did much better on the second set of questions than on the first. This should help them understand that it is people who give richness to life.

Joann Jones demonstrates the importance of seeing people who often go unseen. "During my second month of college, our professor gave us a pop quiz. I was a conscientious student and breezed through the questions, until I got to the last one: 'What is the first name of the woman who cleans the school?' Surely, this was some kind of joke. I had seen the cleaning woman several times. She was tall, dark-haired, and in her fifties, but how would I know her name? I handed in my paper, leaving the last question blank. Just before class ended, one student asked if the last question would count toward our quiz grade.

'Absolutely' said the professor. 'In your careers you will meet many people. All are significant. They deserve your attention and care, even if all you do is smile and say 'hello.' I've never forgotten that lesson. I also learned her name was Dorothy."

At funerals the possessions of the deceased may be mentioned, but most of the time is spent talking about the relationship others had with them.

Ask: What are some of the positive comments you've heard about those who have passed away?

Examples:
"He loved everybody!"
"She was always helping someone!"
"She always had a smile on her face and food on the table!"
"He would give anyone the shirt off his back!"

Ask: What is the #1 thing people like to hear? It's been communicated time and time again, that the most precious sound a person hears is their name. It is something they were given early in life and the heard it over and over again even before they knew how to say it.

Key Truth: People are important because God says so!

We find this truth demonstrated in the following verses:

Matthew 24:1-2: "Jesus came out from the temple and was going away when His disciples came up to point out the temple buildings to Him. ² And He said to them, "Do you not see all these things? Truly I say to you, not one stone here will be left upon another, which will not be torn down."

Matthew 6:23, "Look at the birds of the air, that they do not sow, nor reap nor gather into barns, and yet *your heavenly Father feeds them. Are you not worth much more than they?"*

Luke 12:6-7, "Are not five sparrows sold for two cents? Yet not one of them is forgotten before God. ⁷ Indeed, the very hairs of your head are all numbered. Do not fear; you are more valuable than many sparrows.

Key Truth: Because people are significant to God, they should be significant to us!

Ask: Share an example of someone you've invested your time, energy, or resources into.

Key Truth: It is more important to build memories than it is to build monuments! To build monuments to yourself (bigger houses, more cars, more toys) you must spend the time needed to accumulate enough money to purchase them. The time you spend gathering goods is time you cannot spend with the ones you love. And in the end, your things will not love you, but the people you've invested time in will.

Key Truth: Jesus died for the people on the earth. He DID NOT die for the planet or the things on the planet! Because He was willing to die for people, He set the tone for the attitude of God toward people. We should desire to have the same attitude.

There are two key desires that most people have regarding relationships:
1.) People want to know that they matter.

2.) People want to know that they are needed.

Each of us has the ability to provide for this need. We just need to take time to do it.

In conclusion, we can see where our emphasis should be regarding people and things:

- People show appreciation-Things do not.
- People receive and give love-Things do not.
- People communicate-Things do not.
- People bring long-term peace and comfort-Things do not.
- People share ideas, dreams, and goals-Things do not.
- People instruct us and challenge us to higher ideals-Things do not.
- People need people-Things do not.
- People matter more than things! Are you spending your time with that which matters most?

Progress Is Made Through Struggle

A principle of strength training in known as P.R.E. (Progressive-Resistance-Exercise). With all the advances in the area of strength training, it still comes down to increasing the weight you lift in order to gain strength.

If it was possible for a person to pick up a calf every day for a year the strength gains would be enormous! That is simply because the calf gets heavier as time goes by. They are participating in a progressive-resistance-exercise.

Key Truth: It is strange that we try to protect our children from the things we struggled over but brag that it was these struggles that made us the man or woman that we have become.

Ask: Share with us someone you know who failed before they eventually succeeded.

Facts

- The average American millionaire has been bankrupt, 3.75 times.
- Henry Ford went broke on five different occasions before he finally succeeded.
- Cheese, aspirin, paper towels, and penicillin are the results of some of the world's most famous failures.
- A football expert labeled Vince Lombardi a failure saying "He possesses minimal football knowledge. He also lacks motivation." Lombardi coached the Green Bay Packers: 1959-1967.
- Won the first 2 super bowls and never had a losing season.
- Winston Churchill failed the sixth grade. He twice failed to achieve an elected office during the early 1920's and had little political influence all through the 1930's. But in 1940 he became prime minister of England at the age of 62. Today he is acclaimed as a great leader and hero of World War II.
- John Bunyan spent his adult life in a prison cell-wrote "Pilgrim's Progress"— continuously in print since 1678.

**Notable Quotable**: *"The roots grow deep when the winds are strong."*

Bible Characters that Struggled
A.) Noah: 120 years in building the ark.

Ask: How do you think those in the area looked at him and treated him? (building an ark in the desert?)

B.) Ruth: Met Boaz by gleaning. (Her future was open-ended. She didn't have "The Book" as we do.)

C.) Nehemiah.: 52 days to re-build the wall. (A hopeless situation-Criticism and opposition from those dwelling in and around Jerusalem.)

D.) Romans. 1:8...Romans. 8:1 (The early Christians tried to find their security in staying together in Jerusalem. Persecution broke out to force them to fulfill Romans. 1:8.)

Notable Quotable: "When I look back, It seems to me, All the grief that had to be, Left me when the pain was O'er, Stronger that I was before."
-Unknown

Illustration 1
The "Bio-Sphere" Experiment: A clear dome was built and supplied with all that was needed to sus-

tain life. (water, a mist to water the grass and trees, a garden for food, sunshine, darkness, pollution-free air, the proper temperature, people to cultivate and care for the environment).

However, they found that the trees began to die, and the experiment failed.

Ask: What do you think they were missing?

Answer: WIND. Wind causes trees to bend and sway. This brings about a pumping action bringing water and nutrition up the stem and out to the branches.

Ask: What lesson for our lives can be learned from this.

Notable Quotable: "A certain amount of opposition is a great help to a man, kites rise against, not with, the wind." -John Neal

Ask: How do struggles help us? What struggles have you encountered in your life that have helped you become stronger?

The temptation to resist difficulties is normal and natural. But we must keep in mind that there are great benefits to overcoming tough times. It is in those times that so much growth can occur.

Illustration 2

When storms come, we see a great difference in response between a herd of cows, and a herd of buffaloes. As the thunder booms and the lightning flashes, the tendency of the herd of cows is to scatter and run away from it. This means that when the storm overtakes them, they spend more time in the storm.

The herd of buffalo, however, see the storm coming and run into it. This means that they spend less time in the storm and come out the other side of it sooner.

Ask: What application can you make from this illustration? Have you seen this take place in your own life? If so, share with us what happened.

Notable Quotable: "Troubles are often the tools by which God fashions us for better things." -Henry Ward Beecher

---

Some things that struggles do for us:
- Struggles reveal our character. You are introduced to yourself and get to know yourself better. Struggles cause you to slow down and really evaluate your life and motivations.
- Struggles motivate us to depend on God. Sometimes, the struggles in our lives are

brought through God's intervention. He uses difficulties to drive us to Him.

- Struggles put us in a position to relate to others in their struggle. There is great strength in being able to honestly say, "I know how you feel!"
- Struggles prepare us to overcome lesser struggles. When we face struggles and can look back at bigger obstacles we have overcome, it gives us the confidence we need to press on and not give up.
- Struggles build our testimonies. When we have overcome something, we have the opportunity to share this experience with others and thereby give them encouragement to overcome what they may be going through.

Notable Quotable: *"Life isn't about waiting for the storm to pass...It's about learning to dance in the rain." -Vivian Greene*

Illustration 3

When a caterpillar is in a chrysalis it is maturing into a butterfly. It remains in the chrysalis until it gets to the point when it is strong enough to leave. When it is in the cocoon and grows to be a butterfly, it must struggle to free itself. This movement strengthens its wings and presses fluid out to its wings giving it vibrant colors. Interrupting this struggle ("helping" the butterfly) by opening the side of the chrysalis weakens the insect and shortens its life.

Ask: What application can we make regarding this?

Challenge: Instead of fighting and resisting the challenges and struggles in your life, learn to lean into them and seek to discover how they will eventually be a help to you. The key is to trust God in the midst of the struggle.

About the Author

⚜

Dr. Jirgal is a 1980 graduate of Gettysburg College where he became a four-time conference champion, All-American, and inductee to the Middle Atlantic Conference *All Century Team* in the pole vault. He holds an undergraduate degree in health education and physical education. Following graduation, he taught on the high school and college level while coaching football and track in both venues. He holds masters degrees in health education, sports medicine, and divinity, as well as a doctorate in ministry.

He has been the director of Sports Medicine at Wingate University, area director for the Fellowship of Christian Athletes and has served on the staff of Hickory Grove Baptist Church in Charlotte, N. C., as well as leading Lakeview Baptist Church, in Monroe, N. C. and Anderson Grove Baptist Church as the Senior Pastor. He has served on the local board of directors for the Fellowship of Christian Athletes, the board of trustees at New Orleans Baptist Seminary and the ministerial board of Wingate University. He currently serves on the board of directors for The

Carolina Study Center, and Fathers in Touch ministry.

Dr. Jirgal is the founder and director of *The Jirgal Leadership Institute* where he strives to equip people for success in leadership roles. He and his wife Pam have three children, Joshua, Caleb, and Sarah. They reside in Mint Hill, N. C.

OTHER BOOKS BY DR. STEVEN JIRGAL

The Path of a Champion
Dirty Dozen
Dying to Live
Life Points
Principles of Wholeness
Mining the Mind of King Solomon
Intentional Steps
Encounters with the Christ
The Going to Bed Book

To learn more about the titles above,
visit www.JirgalLeadership.com.

www.ingramcontent.com/pod-product-compliance
Lightning Source LLC
Chambersburg PA
CBHW071828020426
42331CB00007B/1650